Beyond Robert's Rules.
An Overview of Group Communication Models Including Appreciative Inquiry, Restorative Justice, Dynamic Facilitation, NVC Mediation, Intergroup Dialogue, Circles of Trust, World Café and More...

Nelle Moffett with Richard D. Bowers

This book identifies communication patterns which limit group interactions and provides examples of some alternative communication models that can open up more possibilities. This book is not an academic treatise. It is designed as a quick reference guide for professionals who want to increase their repertoire of group process models. The first part of the book presents a discussion of the power of communication models to support creativity, collaboration, and conflict resolution. Without a group process repertoire and vocabulary, people tend to remain bound by a limited set of options that produce a limited set of outcomes.

The second part of the book provides references to a collection of group process models, from basic circle models to self-organizing models for large groups, such as Open Space Technology. Each model is presented with a brief overview, applications, benefits, and a reference to a source for more detailed information.

Effective group process models give voice to multiple perspectives, alternative ideas, or new directions and expand individual participation, responsibility, enthusiasm, creativity, and well-being in the workplace and other settings. The examples of group processes provided in this book can show you a variety of ways to change old, limiting, or ineffective patterns of communication.

**Other Books by Nelle Moffett and
Richard D. Bowers**

Taking Charge of Your Spiritual Path

Happiness is a Good Story

*Empathy in Conflict Intervention: The Key to Successful
NVC Mediation*

Beyond Robert's Rules

An Overview of Group Communication Models Including Appreciative Inquiry, Restorative Justice, Dynamic Facilitation, NVC Mediation, Intergroup Dialogue, Circles of Trust, World Café and More…

Nelle Moffett
with Richard Bowers

Harmony World Publishing
Jerome, AZ

Harmony World Publishing
PO Box 876
Jerome, AZ 86331
Email: info@harmonyworld.net
www.harmonyworld.net

Printed in the United States of America

Trademarks: Nonviolent Communication, NVC, and The Center for Nonviolent Communication are trademarks of The Center for Nonviolent Communication located at 5600 San Francisco Rd. NE Suite A, Albuquerque, NM 87109.

ISBN 978-0-9911117-2-5

Acknowledgments

I feel deep gratitude for all of the facilitators and authors presented in this book. I am grateful for the methods of communication and group processes that they have developed, and for the work they do to support people around the globe in having safe, authentic, and transformative dialogue. I feel grateful for all of you who have picked up this book and for the work that you will do to change the nature of communication within your sphere of influence.

Acknowledgments

Table of Contents

Preface

This book is written by two authors, Nelle and Rick. We enjoy writing together and take on different roles in each book. We believe that using "I," rather than "we," is more personal and connecting with the reader. It is also much less awkward than shifting back and forth from "we" to "I" and creating ambiguity about which one of us is speaking. In this book, Nelle is the primary author using the word "I" to tell her stories from her perspective.

Part 1

When I was learning a new way of speaking (Nonviolent Communication™) that included expressing feelings and needs, I found it difficult to bring this way of speaking into my workplace which valued thoughts, opinions, strategies, and directives. In the first place, given the signals and social norms within this context, I had a hard time even remembering or having access to my knowledge and skills of this new way of speaking, falling easily into the automatic patterns of the workplace. Secondly, when I did remember, I felt extremely awkward and reluctant to speak in this new "weird" way. I also felt afraid of the reactions that I might get if people noticed that I was speaking strangely.

It was only gradually over a period of time that I was able to begin to notice my own feelings in the work environment and to find a way in which I felt safe to express them. Even so, my self-expression did not change the old norms or create new patterns for communication within the groups where I was a participant. Eventually, I developed enough skill and confidence to have an impact in the groups I facilitated and in the relationships I had with individuals I trusted.

Through this experience, I gained awareness of the power of existing communication norms to define roles and limit self-expression. I began to experiment with different communication patterns and create new norms that allow room for collaboration, dialogue, creativity, innovation, safety, and well-being within organizations and relationships. I learned how challenging it can be to disrupt the social conventions, social roles, and communication norms that are consciously and unconsciously entrenched in organizations and relationships. I noticed that people can become very uncomfortable when the game is changed and they do not understand the new rules of the game. Resistance to change is inevitable.

I have realized how much these social norms limit what is possible within organizations and relationships simply because there was no established way to talk about new possibilities. As social beings, we need groups and interactions that support us in becoming more fully ourselves. It is a tragedy of human development when the groups and relationships in which we spend the bulk of our time suppress and restrict the full expression and development of our human potential. It was from my desire to expand human potential within organizations that I became interested in finding ways to disrupt stagnant and ineffective communication norms.

Purpose and Audience

It is my intention in this book to make visible these communication patterns which limit our group interactions and to provide examples of some alternative models that can open up more possibilities.

This book is not an academic treatise. It is designed as a quick reference guide for professionals who want to increase their repertoire of group process models. I learned many of these models over the course of my career. How I would have enjoyed finding a resource such as this book to provide me with an overview of a collection of models from which I could select an approach for my specific needs and audience at the time! The majority of the book will provide a listing and references to a collection of models including a brief overview of each one. This book will not provide you with enough information to learn how to facilitate these models. For this level of detail, at a minimum you will need to go to the source materials themselves.

It is my hope that these examples of alternative communication patterns will expand your awareness of models of communication that can be used for a variety of different purposes. Without a group process repertoire and vocabulary, we tend to remain bound by a limited set of options that produce a limited set of outcomes. The examples of group processes provided in this book can show you a variety of ways to disrupt the old norms of communication and provide a new set of rules that can be learned. Having more communication process tools available will expand your possibilities for communication, collaboration, participation, relationships, and well-being.

I will be referring to these communication norms by using the word "protocol." Synonyms for the word protocol include procedure, etiquette, practice, conventions, code of behavior, and set of rules. According to the Merriam-Webster dictionary, the definition of protocol is

1. a system of rules that explain the correct conduct and procedures to be followed in formal situations
2. a code prescribing strict adherence to correct etiquette and precedence (as in diplomatic exchange and in the military services) <a breach of protocol>.

I will be using the word "protocol" instead of other common words such as "model," "pattern," or "method," in order to call attention to the specific practice that I want to discuss in this book. Sometimes when using a common word, the intended new meaning becomes invisible and a common meaning is assumed. By using the more uncommon word "protocol," I hope to stimulate an awareness of a natural, rule-bound process that is usually invisible in our social interactions. Let me explain what I mean by this.

The Water We Swim In

In our personal relationships and our group processes within organizations there are customs, expected behaviors, norms, and standard assumptions related to how we communicate. These protocols for behavior are important for defining the form and feel of the interaction. The protocols serve to put people at ease by setting boundaries and creating roles and rituals for social interactions. When someone asks you,"How are you?" you do not need to ponder and examine your feelings in order to know how to respond. You quickly and easily respond, "Fine, thanks." There is comfort for both people in that exchange. If someone does not play by the customary social rules and responds with a detailed description of their ailments, the first party will likely feel annoyed and uncomfortable and will be looking for a quick escape route. Communication protocols provide a formula for many social interactions that let us know what is expected, providing comfort and ease for everyone involved.

We are trained very early in life to understand the roles that people play and our place in the group, first in our families, then in school, and in our peer groups. In families, schools, and in our places of work there are usually clear hierarchies and power relationships that must be honored in order to be accepted or included as a member of the group. Stepping outside of these norms can have unpleasant consequences.

Cultural differences. Our cultures of origin contribute to the assumptions and rules for social engagement. The diversity of cultures found in the United States adds complexity to our social interactions and can easily lead to misunderstandings as the rules of one culture are innocently broken by members of other cultures. For example, there is an inevitable culture-clash between Navajo and White cultures because several key rules for etiquette are exactly opposite (e.g., firm vs. soft handshake, eye contact vs. no eye contact). The negative judgments of each party of the character of the other party are silently, unconsciously, and often incorrectly made based on the social rules each one grew up with.

Group membership. Part of the process of entry into a new group is learning the local norms and power structures of that group. These group protocols provide structure for various kinds of communication as well as dictate the kinds of communication that are acceptable in the group. A new member to a group will usually be cautious about saying too much too soon, before taking time to observe the group interactions for acceptable patterns of communication.

Social intelligence involves understanding what to look for in terms of group norms. The rules for informal interactions are not written down anywhere and may be mostly unconscious – until someone breaks a rule. The consequences of breaking a group rule could be ostracism and/or expulsion from the group without the guilty person even knowing what went wrong. Therefore, we learn early in childhood that it is essential for success and survival in group interactions to know the rules of engagement, the communication protocols.

Importance of context. Communication customs are usually driven by the context of the interaction. Sometimes the context is evident by who is participating in the conversation. However, often the same people meet for different purposes. When this occurs, people look for clues to indicate which communication protocol is in effect, such as location, name of the group, group leader, agenda, language cues, or other visible signal. People will automatically and usually unconsciously shift their way of being in the group based on the clues they pick up about which communication protocol is in effect. Protocol clues are therefore extremely important signals that let participants know how they are expected to behave and what role is acceptable for them to play.

For example, we learn the classroom protocol beginning in the first grade. We learn that the teacher is in charge and does all of the talking unless you are called on to speak. You must raise your hand if you want to speak and wait until the teacher calls on you. You must speak only about the topic that the teacher has specified ("How many pages does the paper have to be? ") or to a process (e.g., "May I go to the bathroom?"). Unless specifically asked for a different kind of response, you are to give the response that the teacher is expecting. Now as adults, when we walk into a group meeting where the seats are lined in rows facing a speaker at the front, we are automatically signaled and probably assume that the classroom protocol is operating.

We learn other types of protocols within our families including our first experiences with hierarchical power structures. In families, communication protocols are not as formally defined as in organizations, but they exist nonetheless. For example, each family member has learned a role that provides or restricts access to power in the family, such as father, mother, eldest child, youngest child, stepfather, stepchild, grandmother, favorite child, or black sheep. Family protocols may include decision-making processes, dinner table protocols, asking permission, reprimands, holidays, arguments, and money conversations. These protocols define who gets to speak, specific language patterns, timing, action patterns and rituals, and both formal and informal power structures. Children are naturally adept at picking up subtle cues and manipulating family systems to get their needs met. Despite formal power structures, an observer might notice a dinner table ritual where the two-year old is in complete control.

In relationships between two individuals, there are protocols for courtship, friendships between male/female, male/male and female/female, interactions with neighbors, and interactions with strangers in various contexts. Just as in organizations, these social customs both facilitate and restrict the kind of communication that is accepted in each of these contexts. When one person steps outside of these expected behaviors, the existence or quality of the relationship is potentially at risk. In addition, it usually takes courage on the part of one of the individuals to initiate a conversation for change and such a change of protocol requires agreement of both parties in order for the relationship to continue.

Our places of work also consist of multiple social contexts that have different rules and expectations for behavior. There are many formal and often written communication protocols such as interviewing candidates for jobs, performance reviews, filing grievances, and voting people into elected positions. Robert's Rules of Order is a commonly used protocol for conducting formal meetings. This protocol is useful for maintaining an orderly process, furthering action agendas that have support from more than one person, allowing for focused discussion, voting, and keeping a formal record of proceedings.

Unwritten or informal protocols in a workplace setting may be the norm in various kinds of meetings. Staff meetings may be led by the boss who sets the agenda, whereas collaborative teams are often facilitated by a peer or member of the team. In each of these informal and formal settings, the power structure, format, acceptable topics, forms of expression, and roles of participation are generally understood by members of the group. A person who steps outside of these expected behaviors runs a great risk of being socially shunned, officially punished, or fired from the workplace.

Benefits and Drawbacks of Communication Protocols

This section addresses how to use your knowledge of the power of protocols to facilitate systemic change using the workplace system as an example, although the same principles apply for systems in other contexts as well. I have already discussed how communication protocols are powerful determiners of human behavior. These protocols serve to define and elicit expected and socially accepted behaviors. Protocols are the carriers of culture, whether it is a culture found in an ethnic, religious, family, school, social, or workplace context. When a system of human interaction is in crisis, something about the old way of behaving is no longer working for the well-being or survival of the group. However, *communication protocols are seldom, if ever, identified as part of the problem or as a potential source for a solution.*

While communication protocols are useful for establishing expectations and maintaining order in an organization, they also establish barriers that limit or exclude other forms of communication that might be beneficial for the organization and the well-being of the people who work within it. In my experience, many efforts to introduce change into a workplace system fail because the operating protocols continue to elicit the old patterns of behavior. Changing old behavior patterns requires establishing a new protocol to elicit a new behavior pattern and replace the old pattern. Without establishing a new norm, people will revert to the old norms and these old patterns will prevail. Working consciously with communication protocols can be an effective way to disrupt the old, ineffective norms and replace them with more effective behaviors.

The cost of unexamined protocols. Organizations with unexamined communication protocols and norms may be paying a high price. Organizations with protocols that limit participation and expression risk losing the full participation and engagement of their members. Equally at risk is the leader who does not invite and welcome opposing points of view, and may soon find him/herself, like the fabled emperor, without any clothes on.

For example, employees with low status or minority opinions in the organization often do not have a voice even if these people are present for the conversation. Existing protocols may not provide a welcoming and safe opportunity for them to express alternative or opposing perspectives. Failure to have effective protocols for giving voice to multiple perspectives, alternative ideas, or new directions sadly restricts employee participation, responsibility, enthusiasm, creativity, and well-being in the workplace. Quality circles, which were popular in the 1980's and 90's, were an attempt to install protocols that supported creativity, innovation, and continuous improvement and were successful in organizations where the leadership welcomed and followed through on employee ideas.

Another example of the impact of missing protocols is a lack of either formal or informal communication protocols for addressing conflict. The absence of a specific, supportive, and safe protocol to address conflict often prevents organizations from dealing constructively with conflicts when they arise. Unfortunately, I have seen organizations that rely only on formal grievance proceedings to meet this need. However, by the time a conflict meets the level of a formal grievance, much damage has already been done within the individual, within relationships, and within the overall well-being of the organization.

I am familiar with a case where conflict arose between two co-workers who worked in the same office. The female told her boss that she was uncomfortable with her male co-worker for making unwelcome comments about her being "menopausal." The boss offered to mediate between the two co-workers but the female employee said she would take care of it herself. The female employee then began to make accusations to her boss about her co-worker saying that he was working for other clients while on the job. As a result, the boss set up more strict rules for everyone in the office. Six months later, the female employee went to the grievance officer to complain about her co-worker but refused to file a grievance because she didn't want the grievance officer to talk to her co-worker. The grievance officer told the boss about this but said that this was "confidential" and no action could be taken because a formal grievance had not been filed. The female employee then went to the union to file a complaint against her boss.

This case provides an example of how, without a shared protocol for dealing with conflict, people will default to ineffective and even destructive protocols such as gossip, back stabbing, sabotage, subversion, mutiny, passive aggressive behavior, or withdrawal into compliance. All of the turmoil in this example was created primarily because the organization was averse to conflict and did not have constructive protocols in place to address conflict while it was still small and local. The grievance procedure was too big a step for the female employee to take and involved direct confrontation of her male co-worker. Instead she chose more indirect, subversive, and ultimately more destructive ways to address the conflict.

Challenges to changing old protocols. Bureaucracies are a useful type of organizational structure that implies a set of protocols, such as those that support hierarchical decision-making. This kind of organizational structure is very effective in times of relative stability and slow change. Bureaucracies are designed to resist change; they are designed to create consistency and maintain the status quo. In bureaucracies, protocols and procedures are usually well documented and followed. Tolerance for deviation and creativity is low. Things are typically done the way they have always been done before, whether or not this way is effective.

In bureaucracies, there is seldom an established protocol for creativity and innovation. Bureaucracies also do not handle communication across reporting lines, or "silos", very effectively. All is well, until the world around these organizations begins to change at a faster speed or in unanticipated directions which create a crisis for the organization. The normal and expected response to disruption of protocols in a stable system is to resist change or even to attack the change agent.

Consider the Veteran Administration's "Wait-time" scandal. In early 2012 the incoming director of the Phoenix VA hospital was informed of problems by an emergency room physician. By late 2013, seeing no improvements, a retiring physician went public as a whistleblower. Three years after the original report, with subsequent investigations, top management changes, disparaging media coverage, more whistleblowers, and public official's scrutiny, systemic problems still persisted.

It can be very difficult for a single individual to make changes in the existing social protocols, particularly for an individual whose role does not include this responsibility. Changing social norms within an organization usually requires executive direction, a collaborative process, or intervention from an external consultant, regulatory or accrediting body. Individuals who step outside of the behavioral and communication norms put themselves at risk of marginalization, rejection, or termination from the organization. A poignant example can be found in an April 2015 *USA Today* report where a fired whistleblower at the Tomah Veterans Affairs Medical Center later committed suicide.

It is helpful for change agents to remember that times of crisis, where the survival of the organization is threatened, can provide an opening for change that didn't exist previously, especially for introducing new communication protocols. When it becomes urgent to create a change, it can be very helpful for change agents to understand the power and subtlety of protocols and how to use them for the benefit of organizational change. For the knowledge-able leader, the VA crisis could have provided the perfect opportunity to establish new communication protocols as part of an effort to change the culture.

Structures that protect and support innovation. Recognizing the difficulty of sustaining creative thinking and developing innovative projects within a bureaucracy, Lockheed Martin established a separate entity which was responsible for developing its innovative aircraft designs. This separate group was called "Skunk Works," a name that is recognized in the business world to describe a group within an organization which has been given a great deal of autonomy and freedom from the normal bureaucratic rules and protocols.

Organizations that want to encourage innovation must usually create an entirely different, non-bureaucratic form of structure where the protocols support rather than squelch creativity and out-of-the-box thinking. A little-known but highly significant group that is formed to support innovation and structure is the Internet Engineering Task Force (IETF). This international group develops and promotes operating standards for the Internet. It has no formal business structure, operating almost entirely through volunteers, and is open to anyone who wants to participate. The standards developed by the IETF are voluntarily adopted throughout the world.

The IETF meetings are described as fluid, dynamic, and fun. The IETF accomplishes its role through work groups that each deal with a specific topic. The roles, responsibilities, processes, and protocols are defined in charters which are updated as needed although each group Chair has her/his own style and way of working. These work groups focus on completing a specific task through creative collaboration. Decisions within the work groups are made by "rough consensus." Sometimes a "humming" protocol is used to determine consensus: following prompts by the group Chair, participants hum if they agree with the proposal, or hum if they disagree with the proposal. The Chair decides when the work group has reached rough consensus. Once the task is completed the work group disbands.

Using Protocols for Systemic Change

I have mentioned how protocols can either work against change or serve to support change. Protocol clues or signals are extremely important to notice and replace if you want to disrupt old behaviors and create a new norm. A new norm must contain signals that indicate a shift in context and expectations for what will follow. When there are clear signals of a shift to a different protocol, people will be more likely to follow along easily and naturally. For example, changing the arrangement of the chairs in the room from a classroom arrangement to a circular arrangement will signal participants that there *may* be a new protocol operating.

When protocol signals are unclear or send a mixed message, people will very likely experience confusion and anxiety. Suddenly, they do not know what their role is, what to do, or what to say in order to be accepted and avoid punishment. As social animals, we all have a need to know the rules of the game to ensure acceptance in the group and ultimately our own survival.

In the above example, a change in the arrangement of the chairs will not be enough to change behavior; it is simply an initial signal that something different may be expected. Attendees may hold back from changing their behavior until the usual leader further indicates a change by inviting people to speak and by indicating what changes in the rules she is encouraging. In other words, the leader must articulate a new set of rules, a new protocol. If the leader does not change her behavior as well as the arrangement of the chairs, if she dismisses or criticizes the contributions of the people who speak for example, then the old protocol will prevail.

Introducing a new protocol. A new protocol may need to be introduced carefully. Is it a small, local communication system that will be affected or an organization-wide change? Does the change agent "own" the system and have direct responsibility for its effectiveness? Local systems over which you have direct responsibility are much easier to change than organization-wide systems. However, sometimes a significant change can be made through only subtle adjustments to an existing communication protocol.

Here is an example of an organization-wide change in protocol that was subtle, simple, and had a huge impact. A client had a position as Director of Planning and Effectiveness reporting directly to the CEO. In her role, she was in charge of a system for employee proposals for change. These proposals were processed by a representative group which obtained input from their constituencies and made recommendations to the CEO. The organization suffered from a long history of suspicion, distrust, and lack of collaboration among these groups. Feeding this distrust was a lack of visibility about what happened when an employee proposal was submitted. My client created a very simple change to the communication protocol by publishing a weekly e-newsletter that reported every proposal that was submitted including a copy of the proposal, the status of the proposal, the recommendation to the CEO, and the action taken by the CEO. By making the process visible, the employees began to develop more trust of the administration and a sense of true empowerment through the employee proposal process.

To determine how best to introduce a new protocol, a change agent needs to consider the level of investment in the old, ineffective protocol. If the level of investment is high, if the powerbase of the organization is supported through a particular protocol, or if the culture of the system is highly resistant to change, a change agent must use extreme caution to avoid becoming a martyr and being burned at the stake! Highly resistant organizations may illogically prefer to fail their crisis than to adopt change that is forced or mandated without their acceptance and input. Put another way, some entrenched organizations may prefer and support ineffective and even outright negative members rather than a creative change agent. Sad but true!

Cautious approaches to introducing a new protocol. The strategies for introducing a new protocol must be carefully considered to fit the character of the existing organization. Here is an example of a cautious approach for a system-wide change. This protocol minimizes disruption, threat, and rejection by continuing the old, ineffective protocol throughout the development process.

In a separate initiative, leadership could invite people who want to participate in a "pilot program" to create and test a new process. Consideration should be given to the constituency leaders in the organization and how they want to be included in the process. For example, they may want to appoint "volunteers" from their constituency to serve on a task force to create a new process.

With the support of the executive and constituency leadership, a task force can be formed to design a new protocol to address the crisis in a new way. However, it is not sufficient for the task force to go through a redesign process without bringing the entire organization along with them. I have seen many situations where the task force members go through a meaningful process of discussion, brainstorming, and design, only to hit a brick wall when they introduce their Grand Solution to an organization that has not experienced the same epiphany. (See the Wisdom Council Protocol in Part 2 of this book under Emergent Processes for an ingenious way to address this problem.)

Here is another strategy for helping the organization to keep pace with the task force. During the design phase, the task force can regularly communicate their progress by 1) sending out drafts of the new protocol to the whole organization for input, 2) publicizing the testing process and outcomes, 3) publishing a proposed calendar for turning off the old process and launching the new process, and 4) providing a means for people to provide suggestions and voice concerns about the new protocol. In other words, the task force is advised to create a specific "development communication protocol" for communicating from their group and receiving communications from the larger organization throughout the test process. Then, once the new pilot process has been developed and as a further precaution, the "pilot process protocol" can run parallel to the old process as long as needed for the organization to buy-in before it is implemented as a replacement for the old process.

As a final step, the task force must consider the signals in the organization that elicit and sustain the old protocol and how these can be replaced with new signals that elicit the new rules to the game. It may take some time under the new protocol to observe where there may be confusion caused by mixed messages or outright rejection of the new protocol. When there is systematic rejection of the new protocol, rather than the occasional individual resistance, there may be larger protocols in place that preempt this particular new protocol. One place to look for such a preemptive protocol is in the reward and compensation systems of the organization. As long as these systems support the old protocol, there is not much hope for change. Unfortunately, depending on the will of the organizational leadership, some changes may be only sporadically implemented until there is a change in significant personnel.

The elements of a cautious approach are these: leadership support, minimum disruption of the old system, collaborative process, open communication, and development of new communication protocols, including new signals, which will support the change. Further, a cautious approach is one which minimizes the risk to the change agent who facilitates, but does not own, the process. A healthy dose of patience and celebration of small, incremental success goes a long way in preserving the sanity and well-being of a change agent.

Example Protocol in the Workplace

In Part 2, I will present several existing protocols. However, these and other formal protocols are not your only resource. It is sometimes quite useful to create some small protocols to serve a specific purpose. Here are two successful examples of custom protocols implemented in a small, contained context (not organization-wide).

A client of mine was hired into a company and put in charge of a work process that involved collaboration among multiple departments. This work process had a history of missing deadlines, confusion about responsibilities, poor communication between departments, and blaming individuals in other departments. My client, let's call him Robert, saw the need for a communication protocol that enhanced clarity and collaboration among the departments.

Launching protocol. Robert began the change by creating a new protocol for launching the process. He convened a meeting that included the supervisors and staff of all of the departments involved. In other words, the meeting contained all of the people involved in the process, both those who did the work as well as those who supervised and assigned roles for doing the work. He used a calendar as a tool for clarifying roles and responsibilities.

Robert started off by establishing a target due date one week prior to the official deadline. He then facilitated a conversation among all of the parties present to identify the steps in the process, who did the work for each step, and the timelines needed for each step along the way. Mapping out the process in this way generated cross-department communication and brought forth the interdependencies among the departments. As the group went through each step, they confirmed the people responsible for completing the work as well as lines of communication for requests and handoffs. As each step was identified, the participants negotiated the timeline for completion of each step.

Robert recorded all of this information on the calendar so that the whole group could see the big picture of the flow of work that was needed in order to accomplish the process and meet the target deadline. When the whole group agreed to the project calendar, Robert asked each member to check their personal calendars to make sure that no one had planned to attend conferences or take vacation leave at critical work times. (This was a problem in the past.) Through this conversation, each member of the group was empowered to complete their task and communicate essential information to others within the group.

Debriefing protocol. When the actual task of doing the work was completed by the target due date, Robert convened a meeting of the same people to celebrate the successful on-time (early) completion and to debrief the process. Knowing about the previous conflicts within the group, Robert was sensitive to the need to create a safe space that was free of blame and finger-pointing. He began the new debrief protocol by asking the group to identify what worked in the process that they want to repeat next time. Robert inserted his own observations which acknowledged individual successes that were not mentioned by others in the group.

Robert then asked the group to identify those aspects of the process which did not work so well and needed to be improved for next time. He was amazed to notice that members tended to point out things in their own process that had not worked for them rather than pointing to errors that others had made. He interpreted this as an indication that people felt safe in the conversation. The members were able to support each other in developing strategies that would improve the process in the next iteration. Robert took notes of the successes and areas of improvement and distributed these notes to the entire group.

With each iteration of the process, Robert noticed that collaboration and communication increased, errors decreased, and the deadlines were consistently met. Once the process had settled into a consistent pattern with no further glitches, Robert determined that there was no longer a need to hold face-to-face launching and debriefing meetings because the communication protocol had become the new norm among the group. Instead, Robert sent email with a draft calendar based on the prior iteration, for review and editing prior to the start of each iteration. At the end of the work process, Robert sent email with his congratulations and thanks for a successful process and invited any comments or suggestions for needed improvements. By creating this launching and debriefing protocol, Robert changed the social interaction among this group of people from one of conflict and failure to one of collaboration, communication, and success.

Part 2

In this section I will provide short summaries of a collection of existing group communication protocols, although they are not commonly identified by that name. These examples represent a variety of group processes for different kinds of circumstances and to achieve different goals. From these examples, I hope to provide you with a tool bag of protocols that you can use, modify, or take as inspiration to create your own. These summaries are not intended for training you how to use these protocols. They are merely a resource for you to get a brief idea of different protocols that might be applicable in your situation and to provide you with a primary reference for more detailed information.

Hiring a consultant. These brief summaries may especially be helpful if your organization intends to hire a consultant. Each consultant will have her/his own single or collection of protocols that they use, their own bag of tricks, so to speak. With this book, you will be able to ask key questions and discern which consultants may be a good fit for the needs and culture of your organization. I can tell you how disconcerting it can be to have a consultant come into your organization with a protocol that is either ineffective or disruptive for your organization. It can be either, at a minimum, a waste of valuable funds or, at worst, destructive of something that you have painstakingly built up in your organization.

Empowering yourself as change agent. You can use these summaries to stimulate your creativity to develop your own protocol. Or they might stimulate your interest in seeking more in-depth training in a particular direction to add to your tool belt. In

MARIELOU CIFUENTES
842 JUNIPERO AVE
LONG BEACH, CA 90804-4623

0051
1418

90-8200/3222

PAY TO THE
ORDER OF _Skye Bigan_ $ 1030.00

DATE 11/29/2021

One Thousand Thirty DOLLARS

SCHOOLSFIRST
FEDERAL CREDIT UNION

P.O. Box 11547
Santa Ana, CA 92711-1547
schoolsfirstfcu.org

MEMO _Rent 12/21_

⑆3222 8200⑆ ⑈40 1036 208 708⑈ 0051

any case, these short summary descriptions will only provide you with a general idea of what each protocol has to offer and what situations may benefit from using the protocol. You can then gather more detailed information about the protocols which interest you for a specific situation.

Organization of Part 2. I have grouped these protocols loosely into categories to make them easier to find. However, some of them might also fit within another category just as well. In order to provide an easy-to-use reference guide, I have used a standard structure of four sections for each protocol: 1) A reference to a primary source of information on the specific protocol, 2) the author's verbatim (cut and pasted) description of the protocol, 3) my comments on the appropriate setting and probable outcome or purpose of this protocol as well as the potential benefits, and 4) a very brief summary of the basic procedure.

Small Group Protocols

This set of protocols is especially useful for small groups of two to twenty people. They are relatively easy to facilitate and the rules are easy for people to understand. Sometimes the ground rules for the group process are posted for everyone to see. These protocols can be stand-alone events or can be used as part of a longer interaction or series of interactions which employ other protocols as well. These small group protocols have in common the benefits of creating a safe space and allowing everyone the opportunity to speak. These protocols do not necessarily lead to a decision being made.

Basic Circle Protocol

Worldcat Reference. Pranis, K. (2005). *The little book of circle processes: A new/old approach to peacemaking.* Intercourse, PA: Good Books.

Author's Description. Drawn from Native American practices, these peacemaking circles are used in many communities to deal with conflict and create stronger relationships. Includes detailed information about how to lead and/or participate in one of the circle process. Our ancestors gathered around a fire in a circle, families gather around their kitchen tables in circles, and now we are gathering in circles as communities to solve problems. The practice draws on the ancient Native American tradition of a talking piece. Peacemaking Circles are used in neighborhoods to provide support for those harmed by crime and to decide sentences for those who commit crime, in schools to create positive classroom climates and resolve behavior problems, in the workplace to deal with conflict, and in social services to develop more organic support systems for people struggling to get their lives together.

Setting, Purpose, and Benefit. The basic circle protocol is versatile and can easily be adapted for a variety of contexts, issues, sizes of groups, and purposes. It is a simple process both for people to learn and for leaders to facilitate. The basic circle protocol can provide either an informal or formal protocol ranging from family dialogues to Restorative Justice Circles (included in a later section).

The primary benefit of the basic circle protocol is the opportunity it provides for every person in the circle to speak without interruption, comment, or debate from others. Everyone has an equal turn from the youngest child to the most elevated leader. The basic circle protocol provides an opportunity for everyone to tell their own story from their own perspective.

The basic circle protocol can be used as a first step prior to follow-on protocols which involve dialogue and problem solving. It can also be used as a final step of a longer process to allow the group to find closure and completion. In a heated conflict situation, the basic circle process slows down the action so that all perspectives can be heard and forms the basis for mutual solutions to be developed later. This protocol supports individual self-expression, deep listening, mutual respect, authentic sharing of feelings, needs, and concerns. When everyone's voice has been heard, it becomes easier to move into win-win solutions, team building, and group support.

Basic Procedure.

1. Participants sit in a circle.
2. The circle is convened to discuss a specific topic that is announced by the convener in advance. A facilitator starts the circle by restating the topic and context for the circle.
3. A "talking piece" is often used to indicate who is empowered to speak. The person holding the talking piece is the only one empowered to speak. A talking piece may be an object that has symbolic meaning for the group members or it may simply be a microphone.
4. The facilitator either states or leads the group in generating the guidelines of the protocol.
5. The facilitator is responsible for maintaining the safety of the interaction. The facilitator may be a neutral party or may have some pre-existing status in the group, such as in a family or in a work environment. The facilitator may need to address, either

with the group or in the design of the protocol, how this status might impact the safety and outcome of the group process.

6. Participants speak only from their own perspective and experience. They do not address what someone else has said by giving advice, judgment, or commentary. They may express their own appreciation or concern about another member as well as describe the positive or negative impact that someone else's actions have had on the speaker.

7. If a decision is expected as a result of the circle, the facilitator will describe the guidelines or protocol for how the decision will be made.

8. If confidentiality is a factor for the group, the facilitator will define the expectations and extent of confidentiality and obtain agreement from the group members.

Circle of Trust Protocol

Worldcat Reference. Palmer, P. J. (2004). *A hidden Wholeness: The journey toward an undivided life: Welcoming the soul and weaving community in a wounded world.* San Francisco, CA: Jossey-Bass.

Author's Description. Mapping an inner journey that we take in solitude and in the company of others, Palmer describes a form of community that fits the limits of our active lives. Defining a "circle of trust" as "a space between us that honors the soul," he shows how people in settings ranging from friendship to organizational life can support each other on the journey toward living "divided no more."

<The> paperback edition includes two …useful features. Circles of Trust is a DVD containing interviews with Parker J. Palmer and footage from retreats he facilitated for the Center for Courage & Renewal (www.CourageRenewal.org). *Bringing the Book to Life*, by Caryl Hurtig Casbon and Sally Z. Hare, is a reader's and leader's guide to exploring the themes in *A Hidden Wholeness*. The DVD illuminates and illustrates the principles and practices behind circles of trust. The guide includes questions that connect the DVD to the book, offering "a conversation with the author" as well as an engagement with the text. Together, these features give readers new ways to internalize the themes of *A Hidden Wholeness* and share with others this approach to sustaining identity and integrity in all the venues of our lives.

Setting, purpose, and benefit. This protocol may be used with groups of two to 25 members. The group can meet face-to-face or on a conference call. Meetings may be held weekly, monthly, quarterly, or annually. Meetings may be for 1-2 hours or in a multiple-day retreat format. The purpose of the Circle of Trust is to provide a safe support group for participants to develop the courage to take bold action in one's life, stimulating personal growth and deepening connection with one's inner wisdom.

The protocol provides a structure consisting of five elements: clear limits, skilled leadership, open invitations, common ground, and graceful ambiance. These elements address such things as time commitment, purpose of the group, relational norms and practices to preserve a safe space for the members. A Circle of Trust allows the participants to speak their truths and doubts in their own words and also includes time for silence and deep processing.

Basic Procedure.

1. The facilitator plans the activities of the meeting and usually participates as a member of the group.
2. Divide into small groups of 2-4 members to check in around the question "What has happened in your life since our last gathering that you would like to share?"
3. The facilitator provides a quote, poem, or song to focus the whole group dialogue on a topic or issue. The facilitator uses questions that stimulate individual reflection on what this text stimulates in each individual's inner self. A member's response to a question is a reflection of their own truth and needs no response, endorsement, or correction by anyone else.
4. The whole group dialogue is followed by a period of silence where individual members may walk, reflect, or journal on the topic.
5. Divide into small groups of 2-4 members for each member to speak about whatever they would like to share. All non-speaking members listen without comment during or after a person shares.

6. The whole group gathers again in the large circle and the facilitator invites anyone to speak who wants to share their insights.

Workplace Collaboration Protocol

Reference. Inspired by Miki Kashtan's work through BayNVC.org and expressed in her June 27, 2014 newsletter "The Fearless Heart: Collaboration and Cultural Differences." (For more information see a case study at http://baynvc.org/minnesota-dialogues/, and The Center for Efficient Collaboration at http://efficientcollaboration.org/. Also, search for "collaboration" or "collaborative leadership" on Miki's blog at http://thefearlessheart.org/blog. Contact Miki at mkashtan@baynvc.org.) The text below came from https://www.eventbrite.com/e/convergent-facilitation-learn-how-to-help-groups-make-efficient-collaborative-decisions-tickets-11952635655.

Author's Description. Convergent Facilitation Workshop: Learn how to make efficient collaborative decisions. Other meeting facilitation courses teach participants how to set an agenda, brainstorm, prioritize, and end a meeting on time. But they don't address the underlying reasons most meetings aren't productive -- there isn't enough trust in the room for people to voice their real concerns, the conflicts people have aren't addressed to anyone's satisfaction, and people say they're willing to compromise in the meeting and then sabotage the decision later on. This practical workshop … shows you how to build trust, transcend conflict, and make collaborative decisions without sacrificing productivity.

Setting, Purpose, and Benefit. This protocol would be useful in any collaborative meeting where a particular decision will not be made by a single person in charge (i.e., family, workplace, church, or club). This protocol supports the collaborative environment by taking the needs of all participants into account rather than rushing to closure by going with a majority vote. This protocol allows space for cultural diversity and individual differences to be acknowledged and included in the decision-making process. New solutions may be raised that had not been considered previously. The benefit of taking the time to hear everyone's needs is that silent or minority points of view can be heard and discussed by the group. Ultimately the decision will include everyone's perspectives and therefore will likely avoid unwitting exclusion, resentment, and potential resistance or sabotage of the work of the group. This protocol is based on the principles of Nonviolent Communication™, developed by Marshall Rosenberg, and adapted for a group decision-making process by Miki Kashtan.

Basic Procedure.

1. *How to deal with people who are outliers.* People who see the difficulty and point out problems tend to annoy other people. Rather than excluding outliers, it is helpful to consider them as a gift to the group. If you have only one committee, it is important to have the most difficult people on the committee so that multiple perspectives have a part in the process. They are more likely to point out what has not been considered and to propose more comprehensive solutions. If outliers are not heard, the group may polarize, the outlier may later sabotage the decision, or the solution may fall apart because something important is missing. The larger group is more likely to accept the results when the committee contains diverse perspectives. Ask for volunteers who have strong opinions about this topic, who might have a hard time accepting the outcome of this committee, or who may be concerned that something will be missing if they are not present.

2. *Providing safety throughout the process.* The facilitator needs to protect any dissenters from pressure to make a decision to move forward and interrupt group members who may try to attack or dismiss a minority opinion. The facilitator is willing to hold the group in the uncomfortable space of impasse by pointing out the negative consequences of forcing a decision

that is not fully supported by the group. Very often this impasse can lead to a new breakthrough solution that has not yet been considered.

3. *Agree on principles.* The facilitator listens and collects the non-controversial essence of the issue on the surface detail level, in other words, what is important to the people on each side of the debate. What are the basic principles that they are each trying to meet? The principles explain the "why" underneath the controversial strategies. The principles should state, in positive language, what is wanted in operational terms that apply to everyone. These principles should provide practical criteria for making decisions about strategy. The outcome of Step 3 is a list of principles that everyone can agree to.

4. *Proposal creation.* The committee works with the list of principles created in Step 3 and develops possible solutions to the issue that meet the principles. The solutions are grouped into one or more proposals.

5. *Introducing the next process.* This is where the facilitator makes visible the rules of the operating protocol. Without an introductory statement by the facilitator about the process in Steps 6 and 7, participants may hear these questions as a signal that the common "majority rules" protocol is operating. It could then be more difficult for people who have concerns to voice their concerns. Speaking up may be difficult in a situation of predominant support for a particular direction, especially if there is a pattern in the meeting or organization of going with a majority point of view.

6. *Evaluating the proposals.* Create a table with a list of the principles. The principles now become the criteria for evaluating each proposal. Add two columns labeled "Yes" and "No" to indicate whether the proposal meets or does not meet each of

the criteria. The facilitator might want to begin by saying, "I would like to get a sense of where we each stand on this proposal at the start so that we can explore any concerns we may have." The facilitator may ask, "Who has some concerns about this proposal? And who supports this proposal?" Present each proposal and tally up how many people indicate Yes or No for each of the criteria.

7. *Discussing the proposals.* The facilitator then holds a discussion starting with the proposal with the least amount of objection. The facilitator is not looking for the most popular option but for the option where there are no strong objections. That is why the facilitator starts the discussion process with the proposal where there is the least objection.

8. *Decide on a solution.* Pick one proposal and try to convert it to a decision. The facilitator continues to assess the level of willingness versus dissent and must decide how openly to invite dissent. Here are some probing questions for gauging the level of dissent, without opening too wide of a window, in order to assess when the process is complete. "Is there anyone whose needs would not be met by this proposal?" "Would anyone have a concern if we went forward with this proposal?" "Is there anyone who cannot align with this proposal as it is now written?" Discussion continues until everyone is willing to support the proposal.

Spectrum Decision Making

Reference. McGavin, B. (2015). Spectrum Decision Making - finding consensus through diversity. In *The Focusing Institute Newsletter April 2015.* http://www.focusing.org/newsletter.html.

Author's Description. Forty feisty, opinionated, volatile, caring, passionate people from around the world all in one room. That was what I was walking into with my handful of coloured cards to see if I could help us find a way forward in a difficult and complex situation. Kind of daunting. ...so I took a deep breath and faced the room. My first words were, "This is not about democracy. This is not about majority rule. This is about listening to everyone in the room. This is about including everyone's point of view. This is especially about welcoming and carefully listening to disagreement. In each point of view there is something that we need to take into account to make good strong decisions."

...For three days we talked and discussed and shared and used the cards to find our way forward. We quickly grasped as a group the power of carefully listening to and including opposition, doubt, suspicion and wariness. ... we would easily be able to see that there was someone over there that needed attention and could turn towards them with curiosity and welcome. ... as someone's concerns were addressed, further proposals would arise that were more subtle and nuanced than anything that had been suggested previously and that included and took account of their concerns. In the ensuing discussion, what people hoped would happen if a proposal was adopted became clearer and more articulated so that everyone in the room began to find true common ground. And from that shared understanding the actions taken to make that happen became more flexible and creative.

This is not democracy where the majority rule and the minority feel disempowered. This is about listening carefully to different points of view, to welcoming and championing dissent and diversity of opinion. This is about finding a way forward that is satisfactory to all of the people participating in the decision. Something that is often levelled at consensual decision-making is that the decisions made become the lowest common denominator - full of compromise. Another thing that is often said is that it will take too long to come to an agreement. Neither of these needs to be true - in fact, in my experience, it can be the exact opposite of that. Real, strong, creative decisions that everyone can stand behind can be made rapidly and respectfully.

Setting, Purpose, and Benefit. Ideal for small to mid-sized (50) groups where everyone is easily visible to each other and where there is an issue that can be clearly stated. The intended outcome of the meeting is a decision that the whole group can support. This simple process allows the facilitator and group members to take a quick poll of the group to see where attention is needed to work through an issue. The protocol supports consensus building, hearing different perspectives, and meeting concerns. By providing a simple way to see where there are concerns, the conversation can be enriched and expanded by exploring more deeply into different points of view. In this protocol, people tend to feel comfortable and supported in raising difficult issues. It is easy to get clarification on things that are unclear, to foster creative problem solving, and to empower everyone.

Basic Procedure.

1. Every participant receives a set of colored cards that are big enough for everyone in the room to see at a glance.
2. The cards are printed with some form of the following words by color:

a. White: I need a pause to breathe and reground.

b. Pink (or Purple): I have a proposal for an action.

c. Red: I am not willing for this to go ahead in its present form.

d. Orange: This needs more discussion.

e. Yellow: I have a question; I need something clarified.

f. Green: I am at least 80% happy with the proposal. Or put another way, I am willing to go ahead with the proposal as it stands.

g. Blue: I need someone to listen to how this issue is for me because feelings are arising.

3. The group members use the cards to communicate throughout the process to each other; the facilitator is not the focus. People use the cards throughout the process mostly without being called on formally. What is important in this process is that everyone can see at a glance what everyone else needs in order to move forward.

4. When there is a clearly stated proposal for action, the facilitator (or someone in the group) may call for a poll using the cards.

5. The results of the poll allow the group to quickly see where each participant stands related to the proposal and where to probe for input, clarity, objections, and unmet needs. The facilitator's role is to ensure that anyone with a non-green card gets the attention they need.

6. The goal is to achieve all green cards once a broad spectrum of views has generated a proposal that is agreed upon by everyone in the room without compromise.

Quaker Business Meeting Protocol

Web Reference. http://www.qis.net/~daruma/business.html

Author's Description. *'Quaker business'* is a general term which covers items such as membership, finance, the concerns of individual Friends in relation to the Society and its work, as well as relations with other organisations. <sic> Quaker business meetings are held regularly.... Monthly Meeting is the principal meeting for business and deals with membership, property, finance, appointments, arrangements for Quaker weddings etc....

Friends' business meetings are quite unlike other business meetings you might have experienced. Their form differs from that of a debating society or a union or board meeting. Their form is also liable to vary in detail from one monthly meeting to another. There is a form to it, but it is a flexible one, sensitive to the needs of the individual meeting. Perhaps a Friends' business meeting can be described as an exercise in attentiveness, in listening to the promptings of the Spirit. The overriding need is to discern the will of God in the meeting, and business meetings should be conducted with that fundamental aim in mind.

Setting, Purpose, and Benefit. This protocol provides an opportunity for reflection and prevents anyone from monopolizing the meeting. This protocol may fit the needs of groups who share spiritual values and who want to overtly include their spiritual connections in their group process. The protocol allows space and time for all perspectives to be voiced. It does not rush to a conclusion and historically for the Quakers, even allowing years to elapse if there is no clear direction that emerges from the group. This protocol does not seek consensus but rather seeks clarity in spiritual guidance, or higher wisdom that is recognized by the group, even if all members are not in agreement. After ample opportunity for full self-expression, all members do agree to set aside their personal perspectives, if necessary, because there is a shared value found in spiritual direction.

Basic Procedure.

1. The meeting begins with silence and silence is maintained between individual contributions.

2. The Clerk of the Meeting facilitates but does not lead the meeting or express a point of view. The Clerk summarizes the agenda, provides any necessary background information, and opens the first item before the meeting.

3. People who wish to speak raise their hand and wait to be called on by the Clerk.

4. It is expected that members bring an open state of mind, willing to listen to others' arguments. Members may express contradictory views, but do not argue with one another in meeting.

5. The Clerk helps those present discern the "sense of the meeting" and the prompting of Spirit - which is different from consensus.

6. The Clerk is responsible for drafting a statement reflecting the sense of the meeting and reading it aloud in the meeting where those present can verify the wording and accuracy. If necessary, the minute <sic> is rewritten by the Clerk and presented again to the group before the meeting ends.

7. The minute records the decision of the meeting on a given topic and the collective spirit of the group. In all cases, the meeting must unite in agreement on the minute.

8. If a "sense of the meeting" does not emerge, the issue will remain open for further discussion, even for years, until there is a clear sense of the movement of Spirit on the issue.

Restoring Community and Personal Relationships

This set of protocols is especially useful for small groups of 2 to 20 people. The specific purpose is to address and resolve conflict or some action which has brought damage to another person, property, or community. The intention is to restore relationships and to make amends for any harm that was brought to others. These protocols require skillful facilitators who have received specific training. These protocols have in common the benefits of creating a safe space to address difficult issues which are usually highly emotionally charged. They provide facilitated support for each individual to speak from their perspective. The purpose goes beyond conflict resolution to include perspective taking, shared responsibility, restored relationships, making amends, and creating action steps going forward.

Restorative Justice Protocol

Worldcat Reference. Zehr, H. (2002). *The little book of restorative justice.* Intercourse, PA: Good Books. See also http://www.restorativecircles.org.

Author's Description. Vengeance and bitter violence have had their turns -- without redemptive results. How should we as a society respond to wrongdoing? When a crime occurs or an injustice is done, what needs to happen? What does justice require? Restorative justice is a process to involve, to the extent possible, those who have a stake in a specific offense and to collectively identify and address harms, needs, and obligations, in order to heal and put things as right as possible. Howard Zehr ... proposes workable Principles and Practices for making restorative justice both possible and useful. First he explores how restorative justice is different from criminal justice. Then, ... Zehr presents Restorative Justice Practices. ... This is a handbook, a vehicle for moving our society toward healing and wholeness. This is a sourcebook, a starting point for handling brokenness with hard work and hope. This resource is also suitable for academic classes and workshops, for conferences and trainings.

Key questions:

1. Who has been hurt?
2. What are their needs?
3. Whose obligations are these?
4. Who has a stake in the situation?
5. What is the appropriate process to involve stakeholders in an effort to put things right?

Setting, Purpose, and Benefit. This protocol is used by the criminal justice system for various purposes; however it can also be adapted for families, schools, churches, workplaces, and other environments where a wrongdoing by a member of the community has an impact on the whole group. As a protocol, restorative justice provides a framework for addressing wrongdoing as a way to build and heal relational communities.

The restorative justice protocol involves a direct, facilitated, face-to-face encounter between a victim and an offender with adequate preparation, safeguards, and support. The restorative justice protocol includes all of the stakeholders of a wrongdoing rather than focusing only on the offender. It acknowledges that a wrongdoing is not only a violation of the victim but also of interpersonal relationships within the community. The primary purpose of the restorative justice protocol is to promote healthy communities by making amends for the wrong that has been done and to restore the offender into the community.

The restorative justice protocol provides an alternative for the "punishment protocol." The focus of the protocol is on victim needs and offender responsibility for repairing the harm. Offenders are provided with a supportive environment in which they can acknowledge and take responsibility for what they did. The protocol provides an opportunity for offenders to understand the impact of their actions on others and to encourage them to put things right as much as possible. Community members provide support for the offender to make amends as well as examine any conditions in the community that may have contributed to the wrongdoing, recognizing that everything is interconnected.

Basic Procedure.

1. Identify a facilitator who can remain neutral, maintain safety and respect in the process, and guide the group through the steps of the process.

2. Victim tells offender the impact of the offense and has the opportunity to ask the offender questions.

3. Offender has the opportunity to tell his/her story and to take responsibility for his/her actions.

4. The community members have an opportunity to speak to how the offense has impacted them as members of the community.

5. The offender, victim, and community members negotiate a consensual plan of action that is achievable and realistic for the offender to make amends.

6. Community members identify how they will support and encourage the offender in making things right and how they will follow-up to ensure that the plan is implemented.

7. The action plan includes how the victim and the offender will be reintegrated into the community in a way that restores the well-being of the victim, offender, and community.

8. All aspects of the process are based on mutual agreement rather than imposed by authority.

Third-Party Mediation Protocol

Reference. Bowers, R. & Moffett, N. (2012). *Empathy in conflict intervention: The key to successful NVC mediation*. Jerome, AZ: Harmony World.

Author's Description. The focus of this book is on mediation, a third party intervention role that can be undertaken by supervisors, managers, human resource professionals, marriage and family therapists, teachers, mediators, peace keepers, and parents. The authors make a strong case for the central role of empathy in promoting a successful mediation, especially when ongoing relationships between the parties are at stake. This book provides a thoughtful study of the important role of empathy in mediation through the development of a theoretical model to explain the effectiveness of Nonviolent Communication™ (NVC) mediation. The theory building process used in this book, as well as the list of conditions for a successful mediation, can be broadly applied to other third party intervention methods.

Setting, Purpose, and Benefit. This protocol is useful for conflicts between two people or two perspectives held by small groups of people. This protocol can be used in a variety of settings. Children have been taught a simplified form of this protocol to act in the role of mediator in playground conflicts. This protocol has also been used in settings of serious world conflicts such as the middle-east, Africa, and Ireland. It can also be used in a therapeutic context for conflicts between couples or family members.

The mediator is an active facilitator and role model of the process, maintaining a safe environment and neutrality towards both parties. The mediator models the protocol of listening for each side's feelings and needs and reflecting these back to ensure that they have been accurately heard. The mediator provides support to both parties in making clear "do-able" requests and making agreements that meet the needs of both parties, holding this purpose as the intended outcome of the interaction. The primary benefit of this protocol is in supporting an intention for an ongoing relationship between the parties rather than accomplishing any specific strategy for conflict resolution, thus going beyond negotiation or compromise. When the parties are able to hear and reflect back the needs of the other party, there can occur an opening of the heart that allows for new win-win strategies to be mutually discovered.

Basic Procedure.

1. Mediator asks who wants to speak first. Mediator empathizes with person A and especially reflects back the needs that the mediator heard expressed implicitly or explicitly.

2. Mediator asks person B to reflect back person A's needs.

3. Steps 1 and 2 are repeated until person A has been fully heard.

4. Mediator asks person B to speak next. Mediator empathizes with person B and especially reflects back the needs that the mediator heard expressed implicitly or explicitly.

5. Mediator asks person A to reflect back person B's needs.

6. Steps 4 and 5 are repeated until person B has been fully heard.

7. Mediator invites both parties to make requests of the other party and to strategize solutions and agreements that meet both parties' needs.

8. Go back to steps 1-6 if requests lead to either party becoming emotionally triggered or renewed conflict for either party.

Interracial Dialogue

The specific purpose of the protocols in this section is to build understanding of different perspectives on highly charged topics, develop cross-difference competency, and increase the capacity for authentic self-examination and sharing. These protocols require skilled facilitators who have received specific training. Each of these three protocols has in common the benefits of creating a safe space to address difficult issues which are usually highly emotionally charged. They provide facilitated support for each individual to speak from their perspective.

I begin this section with an example of a generic dialogue protocol that can be used in small or large diverse groups on any variety of difficult or controversial topics. The next two protocols are targeted for conversations about race in small, multi-racial groups, especially within educational settings. These protocols are included here because they address a vitally important issue in our world today, build skillfulness in bridging the gaps across racial groups, and provide access to cultural competency which is an essential skill for achieving connection, understanding, and peaceful relationships.

The Intergroup Dialogue protocol uses a group study model based on a structured curriculum of reading articles and texts, dialogue, and an action project over a standard school semester. The practice of "dialogue about the dialogue," described at the end of this section can be a useful protocol to add to any group process to assess the effectiveness of the group interaction.

The Courageous Conversations protocol is intended to follow an intensive 2-3 day workshop which serves to build awareness of systemic racism and white privilege. From the base of this awareness-building workshop, the protocol supports an authentic dialogue that can go beyond denial, defensiveness, blame, guilt, and anger and begin to form the basis for collaborative, systemic change. The material in this protocol may be useful for skilled facilitators to adapt for other appropriate contexts outside of a school setting.

Dialogue for Difficult Subjects

Worldcat Reference. Schirch, L., & Campt, D. W. (2007). *The little book of dialogue for difficult subjects: A practical, hands-on guide*. Intercourse, PA: Good Books.

Author's Description. The word "dialogue" suffers from over-use, yet its practice is as transforming and as freshly hopeful as ever. Authors Schirch and Campt demonstrate dialogue's life and possibilities in this clear and absorbing manual: "Dialogue allows people in conflict to listen to each other, affirm their common ground, and explore their differences in a safe environ-ment." Schirch has worked throughout the Southern hemisphere in peacebuilding projects. Campt has focused on racial and class reconciliation in American cities.

Setting, Purpose, and Benefit. The dialogue protocol can be used with mid-sized to very large groups. It is important to ensure that all the stakeholders and all the perspectives on the topic are present in the dialogue. In large groups which are broken up into multiple small subgroups, it is important to ensure diversity within each subgroup. Group dialogue for difficult topics requires a trained and skillful facilitator or team of facilitators to create a safe and successful experience for everyone. The dialogue should have a clear topic and intended outcome which are announced in advance.

This protocol provides an opportunity for all participants to express their perspectives in an environment which supports careful and considerate listening. This protocol can help to build a sense of community and understanding among diverse perspec-tives. It can also overcome many of the pitfalls of a typical town meeting or controlled public hearing. For many people, a facilitated dialogue around a difficult topic may be the only opportunity they have had to feel safe enough to really listen to people who have a different perspective on the issue and to honestly express their own point of view without fear of reactions that they are not able to handle on their own.

The facilitated dialogue protocol has many benefits including opportunity for all voices to be heard; creation of relationships which increase the possibility of collaborative action; eliminating grandstanding, accusations, escalation of entrenched positions; opportunity to hear the experiences of participants which have led to their different perspectives on the same issue; opportunity for inquiry into different points of view; opportunity to question one's own opinion and develop a broader perspective without losing face; opportunity for creative thinking around possible actions that may not have been considered before; and going beyond either-or thinking.

Basic Procedure. Successful dialogues can have many variations but usually include these four general aspects.

1. *Establish common norms or ground rules.* I understand this step as a means of making visible the operating protocol. When people understand the rules to the game, they are more able to feel comfortable with their role, they understand what behaviors are accepted (and unacceptable), and they are clear about the intended outcome of the process.

2. *Share personal experiences and perceptions.* A dialogue is not a theoretical, intellectual, or philosophical discussion or an adversarial debate. Instead, a dialogue is expected to be first person accounts of feelings, beliefs, stories of personal experiences, points of view, disappointments, and hopes for the future.

3. *Explore both commonalities and diversity.* In a dialogue on difficult topics, it is important to seek out and allow expression of both areas where participants agree and areas where they

disagree. People are supported in expressing their personal views with acceptance and respect for their perspectives.

4. *Explore possibilities for action.* As participants reveal and explore areas of agreement and disagreement, new possibilities for action are encouraged and discussed. It needs to be made clear at the beginning of the dialogue whether there is an intention to arrive at agreement about action steps by the end of the process or whether the dialogue is a preliminary step for finding a variety of possible actions. An expectation for arriving at an action plan will place a certain pressure on the process. This pressure may be useful in some circumstances and counter-productive in others. The facilitator also must make it clear who is empowered to make action plans or approve recommendations for action that may emerge from this dialogue.

Intergroup Dialogue

Worldcat Reference. Zu'niga, X. (2007). *Intergroup dialogue in higher education: Meaningful learning about social justice.* San Francisco, Calif: Wiley Subscription Services at Jossey-Bass.

Author's Description. Intergroup dialogue promotes student engagement across cultural and social divides on college campuses through a face-to-face, interactive, and facilitated learning experience that brings together 12 to 18 students from two or more social identity groups over a sustained period of time. This volume outlines the theory, practice and research on intergroup dialogue. It also offers educational resources to support the practice. It is a useful resource for faculty, administrators, student affairs personnel, students and practitioners for implementing intergroup dialogues in higher education.

Setting, Purpose, and Benefit. Intergroup Dialogue (IGD) was designed specifically for use on college campuses to promote cultural competence. Sessions are led by trained co-facilitators and follow a curriculum that integrates cognitive, affective, and behavioral components. By following a curriculum of reading materials, structured activities, and reflective dialogue over a semester, the sessions provide practice in a communication protocol which changes the rules of engagement to go beyond the polite, superficial, and circumspect conversations toward reflective, meaningful, and honest engagement across social groups. The group explores the commonalities and differences between the social identity groups under investigation and represented by the membership: race, gender, sexual orientation, social class, religion, or political affiliation. Group interaction promotes "active, generative, and transformative connections and exploration among participants."

Basic Procedure. Intergroup Dialogue is a curriculum using multiple methods and tools rather than a single procedure like the other protocols included in Part 2 of this book. As such, it can be a rich resource for a variety of experiential learning activities and methods for stimulating critical thinking and authentic, respectful dialogue. Facilitators and participants are both trained in the building blocks of dialogue (as opposed to debate) which include suspended judgment, deep listening, identifying assumptions, reflection, and inquiry. Participants explore their social identities through telling their personal story.

I will select only one aspect of Intergroup Dialogue to highlight because it has the most bearing on communication protocols. The authors identify four communication processes which contribute to the ability of participants to create a bridge across their differences.

1. *Appreciating Difference.* The IGD process provides regular opportunities for participants to hear different points of view and different life experiences among the diverse groups reflected among the participants through their structured dialogues.

2. *Engaging Self.* Learning about the "others" in the group is made possible because each participant is willing to share their own perspectives and to re-examine them in light of the group interaction.

3. *Communicating about critical self-reflection.* The IGD process encourages each participant to examine their own ideas, experiences, and perspectives within the context of their identity-group status or privilege, inequality, and oppression.

4. *Building alliances.* The IGD context of regular, small-group meetings over a semester provides the opportunity for emotional and intellectual bonding within the group as well as working together with group members on action projects. The

educational context provides an opportunity for requiring participants to complete action projects related to social justice.

Dialogue about the Dialogue

As a check on the quality of the dialogue process within the group, the facilitator may initiate a "dialogue about the dialogue." This protocol supports group reflection and examination to uncover any hidden dynamics that may be constraining the initial dialogue about diversity. As a result of this inquiry, the group may choose to revisit their group process guidelines, choose to add some new guidelines, or decide to change some aspects of how they work together. This practice of "dialogue about the dialogue" can be a useful protocol in itself to add to any group process. The group addresses the following or similar questions.

1. How are we communicating as a group?

2. What is working?

3. What is not working?

4. Are there any dynamics or tensions that you have noticed that affect your ability to participate fully?

5. What are some ways we are using or not using our dialogue skills?

Courageous Conversations

Worldcat Reference. Singleton, G. E., & Linton, C. (2006). *Courageous conversations about race: A field guide for achieving equity in schools.* Thousand Oaks, CA: Corwin Press.

Author's Description. Singleton looks at the achievement gap through the prism of race, and in "Courageous Conversations About Race"; he begins by examining the evidence that points to race - not poverty - as the underlying cause behind the achievement gap. This work, while exploring how race affects all educators, declares that we need to have engaged, sustained, and deep conversations about race in order to understand students and the achievement gap. Singleton calls this process "courageous conversations." Through these "courageous conversations," educators can learn how to redesign curriculum and create community and true equity. Action steps to close the achievement gap include creating an equity team and collaborative action research. The final chapter presents a system wide plan for transforming schools and districts, including activities, exercises, and checklists for central office administrators, principals, and teachers.

Setting, Purpose, and Benefit. This book, and the processes described within it, provides a strategy for discussing race openly, safely, and authentically specifically in a school environment. Singleton provides a foundation to break the silence about the impact of race, especially for educational leaders who are willing and ready to take effective steps toward educational equity in student achievement. Singleton provides guidance in how to engage faculty and staff in discussions about the impact of race in the classroom and curriculum as a first step in closing the racial achievement gap.

The process of engaging in interracial conversation about race requires a skilled facilitator or multi-racial team of facilitators and could possibly be adapted for other settings besides schools. This strategy provides support for examining racial identity, including white identity, and to discuss the impact of race in one's own life as well as in society. The protocol described below allows each person to express how they have personally experienced the impact of race and to be heard respectfully. Through these conversations, participants have the opportunity to deepen their understanding of the perspectives of others and to be better equipped to recognize and address systemic racism. Deep, effective, interracial dialogue can lead to a transformed racial philosophy through which policies, structures, and practices can be redesigned to truly work toward systemic equity.

Basic Procedure. The **Four Agreements of Courageous Conversation** ensure that participants remain personally engaged, honest, and committed to staying in the conversation.

1. To stay engaged
2. Experience discomfort
3. Speak your truth
4. Expect and accept non-closure

The **Six Conditions of Courageous Conversation** provide a guide through the process of interracial dialogue in a way that promotes safety, depth, and understanding. Singleton's book provides much more variety and depth of issues that can be addressed within each of these six conditions than I can recreate in this brief summary.

1. *Establish a racial context that is personal, local, and immediate.* Begin with an examination of oneself rather than others. Focus on one's own racial consciousness, attitudes, beliefs, identity, and experiences.

2. *Keep the spotlight on race while acknowledging the broader scope of diversity and the variety of factors that contribute to a racialized problem.* The challenge is to resist the temptation to shift the conversation to other diversity-related topics instead of race, such as socio-economic status, gender, family values, education, etc., because these topics are more comfortable for many people to talk about.

3. *Engage multiple racial perspectives by acknowledging the social construction of knowledge.* This condition acknowledges the process through which the meaning of race is created, inherited and interpreted. Engaging with this condition supports the development of skill and capacity to listen to differing perspectives and to engage with differing experiences.

4. *Keeping us all at the table by consciously monitoring the elements of conversation that maintain safety for everyone.* Just being able to talk about race is a significant challenge to overcome given that race is a "hot button" topic. Bringing out conflicting racial viewpoints can increase discomfort and stimulate a reaction to disengage from the conversation. It is especially important to acknowledge different cultural communication styles and expectations as well as balancing power differences among participants. This condition highlights the importance of creating formal guidelines for what participants talk about, how long, skills for listening, and noticing who is and is not speaking. Unstructured conversations about race are rarely successful.

5. *Establish agreement about a working definition of race that clearly distinguishes it from ethnicity and nationality.* While it might be easy, for some people, to think that we all understand what race means, this is not really the case. Actually one's personal understanding of race is very much conditioned by the

individual and cultural context in which one has lived. Race is not just a label for physical and genetic characteristics, but is a complex social and political construction of meaning with different impacts for different people. For example, how is a multi-racial identity experienced in a family and in society? A discussion of the definition of race serves to make the complexity of this topic more visible for all participants. Furthermore, this discussion puts the topic of race front and center instead of dodging, assuming, stereotyping, or beating around the bush. To fulfill the second condition above, race must be distinguished from nationality, ethnicity, and culture.

6. *Examine the presence and role of Whiteness, its impact on the conversation, and the problems being addressed.* A conversation about race cannot begin until the **invisibility** of Whiteness has been addressed. Many White people begin from a place of not being aware of Whiteness as a race. For them, race means Blacks, Hispanics, and Asians and therefore many Whites do not see themselves as having a racial identity. Whiteness defines the dominant culture in the United States and therefore the point of reference for White people is also invisible; for them, it is simply what is normal. Furthermore, many Whites are not aware of the automatic social privilege they receive simply because of their whiteness and will often deny that they have any privilege at all. Interracial dialogue cannot succeed until the role of Whiteness is explicitly addressed and the White participants are able to see their White culture and identity.

Emergent Processes

The protocols in this section are effective in large groups, whole organizations for organizational development and transformation, whole systems for inclusion of all aspects of a problem, and for community organizing efforts that involve multiple entities. These protocols are characterized by the creation of transformative energy that has been described as "unstoppable," "transformative," "inspiring," "engaging," and "empowering." The term "emergent" refers to the way that these protocols allow the unexpected, creative, innovative, convergent, divergent, impossible solutions to emerge from the group process. One could say that the category of Emergent Processes is the latest evolution of brainstorming, and much more.

I believe that each of the following authors would agree about the importance of increasing our capacity to engage in and lead meaningful and productive conversations on interpersonal, group, and system-wide levels. Some authors have identified this capacity as the number one skill required among leaders of all levels in our world today. In addition to the ability to initiate and facilitate such conversation, there is an expectation, certainly among participants, that the conversations will lead to change.

Sustainability is the current new awareness and imperative, and this includes sustainability of the change initiatives in our organizations. It is not enough, for example, to walk our employees through a change process and then to leave them unsupported afterwards. Individuals and groups do not exist in a vacuum, each being a part of a larger system that either empowers or disempowers them. Of what use is it to spend resources on a change initiative if all traces vanish within a week, a month, a year? While the skills for helping a group engage in a creative and generative process are vitally needed, it must also be recognized that people will expect to see lasting fruits of their efforts or they will quickly become cynical and non-responsive to any subsequent requests.

On the other hand, many people in leadership or management positions believe that they must be in control or in charge of their organization. The quality of emergent protocols is the opposite of control and can be experienced as frightening or threatening by those who insist on control, on their plan, or their specific outcome. Clients who are considering an emergent protocol must understand that it is impossible to know exactly how things will turn out. It is not unusual for the cherished rules, plans, and outcomes to be set aside in order to allow a breakthrough idea to emerge. The leadership of the organization must be fully informed of this characteristic of emergent processes and willing to go forward. Otherwise, these protocols are not appropriate for this organization.

Rosa Zubizarreta explains that Jim Rough, creator of Dynamic Facilitation, was looking for a way to help employees at a sawmill find practical solutions for "impossible-to-solve" problems through collective breakthroughs in their thinking. Zubizarreta affirms that "implementation is rarely an issue, given the high energy and commitment that are a natural part of the group's shared discoveries." Cooperrider et al. say about Appreciative Inquiry, "When inspired by a great dream we have yet to find an organization that did not feel compelled to design something very new and very necessary."

Harrison Owen says that Open Space Technology continually demonstrates the emergence of effective leadership and high performance. "Without special preparation and despite all predictions to the contrary, effective leadership, in a mode vastly different from the standard model, happens. Not just occasionally. Not just serendipitously, but in thousands of situations for millions of people over the course of twenty years – it happens.... When you are able to accomplish in two days what you absolutely knew would take ten months, I believe it fair to say that we are in the presence of genuine high performance."

About World Café, Juanita Brown says, "Through our conversations the stories and images of our future emerge.... Our very survival as a human community... may rest on our creative responses to the following questions: How can we enhance our capacity to talk and think more deeply together about critical issues facing our communities, our organizations, our nations, and our planet? How can we access the mutual intelligence and wisdom we need to create innovative paths forward?"

I came across a quote on Facebook which said. "When I die, I hope it is at a staff meeting or staff training because the transition from life to death would be so subtle." Why do we put up with this sense of deadness in our organizations? It doesn't have to be that way. The protocols in this section provide one means of bringing more life into our workplaces, to have conversations that matter, carry life energy forward, and bring people to life. So, fasten your seatbelt and prepare to be energized!

Open Space Technology

Worldcat Reference. Owen, H. (2008). *Open space technology: A user's guide*. San Francisco, CA: Berrett-Koehler Publishers.

Author's Description. What if you could identify a mission-critical issue for your organization, bring together the people with something to contribute and something at stake, focus on that issue and take decisive action all in the same meeting? A fantasy? Not with the application of Open Space Technology. Open Space Technology is a methodological tool that enables self-organizing groups of all sizes to deal with hugely complex issues in a very short period of time. Authored by the originator, the book *Open Space Technology, Open Space Technology: A User's Guide* details what needs to be done before, during, and after an Open Space event. It is the most authoritative book available on how to plan and run a successful Open Space event. This 3rd edition adds a survey of the current status of Open Space Technology around the world, an updated section on the latest available technology for report writing (a key aspect of the Open Space process), and an updated list of resources.

Setting, Purpose, and Benefit. Open Space Technology (OST) is an effective protocol for meetings of between 5 and 2,000 participants. OST empowers self-organizing groups to deal with complex issues in a very short period of time where the answer is not already known and there is a willingness to let go of control. OST has been used effectively by governmental entities to convene stakeholders, citizen groups, agencies, and lobbyists around controversial issues. In fact OST is an effective protocol for uniting groups with enormous diversity in multiple areas such as race, education, social economic status, power position, language, and political perspectives and who may even be historical enemies.

OST is a no-frills protocol that produces fast results (1-3 day workshop) with minimal pre-conference planning involving only logistical details, and requires only one facilitator. The convener identifies a central task for the group (i.e., how to spend $1.5 billion designated for highway construction on tribal and public lands) but does not set an agenda for the workshop. The process quickly engages people on topics that they identify which are related to the central task and that they are passionate about. OST has been used on issues such as product design, strategic planning, community organizing, corporate redesign, national redesign, environmental planning, organizational renewal, professional development, thematic issues, team building, corporation mergers, and event planning.

Basic Procedure.

Five Conditions for Appropriate Use and Success of OST

1. There is a real business issue to work on that can be defined in concrete terms.

2. The issue has to be complex, even "impossible."

3. Participants must be diverse in terms of perspectives on the issue.

4. Participants must be passionate about the topic.

5. The issue must have some urgency for its resolution.

Implementing Open Space Technology

1. Send out an open invitation to the event that identifies the issue, the importance for the future of the organization or community, and what the workshop is intended to accomplish. Participation must be voluntary. People must care about the issues and want to participate in the process.

2. The meeting room is set up in a circle or set of concentric circles. Breakout spaces are provided either in the same room or separate rooms. The facilitator prepares the needed signs, prepares an empty wall for the bulletin board with the Space/Time Matrix and the Daily Schedule, and provides all of the supplies that are needed for the process.

3. The facilitator prepares the Space/Time matrix on the wall ahead of time with a matrix of sticky notes, each with a specific location and time printed on it.

4. The facilitator initiates the workshop by explaining the focus, the process, the schedule, and the work to be done, and then gets out of the way.

5. Anyone who is passionate about one or more issues related to the theme is invited to take responsibility for convening a group to discuss this issue. The convener does not have to be an expert on the issue. After the facilitator has described the process and says, in effect, "Go!" the action shifts to the participants and the facilitator gets out of the way.

   a. Each person who wishes to convene a group steps into the center of the circle, announces their issue and their name, grabs a blank piece of paper for each issue and a marker.

   b. The convener writes the title of the issue/session on the paper and their name.

   c. On the way to the wall, the convener selects a sticky note from the Space/Time Matrix that has a location and time for the session and attaches that to the Issue/Session paper, posts this paper in the designated area on the wall, and returns to their seat.

   d. Within a short period of time, the group has thus self-organized an agenda around topics they are passionate about and have made a public commitment to take responsibility for convening a discussion group on this topic at a specific time and location.

e. People will naturally begin to sign up for sessions at the wall. Even in very large Open Spaces, experience has shown that participants are able to quickly find what they are looking for among the posted issues.

6. Conveners are responsible for entering their group report(s) into a computer.

7. Reports are posted on a designated physical or electronic bulletin board once they are entered and participants receive a printed copy of all reports at the end of the workshop.

8. Action may or may not be an intended outcome of the workshop. However, when people are passionate about an issue and invest time discussing it in-depth with others, they are more likely to accept responsibility for following through on the ideas that emerge. There is a greater likelihood of action when the entire system is included in the workshop because there is no need to go outside of the group for resources or authority to act. The "decision-makers" are involved in the conversation. It also often happens that the immediate next steps are taken even before the end of the workshop. Another option is to open a new space for actionable items to be discussed. The key is to arrive at a common understanding about how the energy created during the Open Space can keep moving forward.

9. Closing Ceremony – passing the "talking stick" or microphone around the circles provides an opportunity for everyone to share briefly what the Open Space workshop has meant to them.

Appreciative Inquiry

Worldcat Reference. Cooperrider, D. L., Sorensen, P. F., Whitney, D., & Yaeger, T. F. (2000). *Appreciative inquiry: Rethinking human organization toward a positive theory of change.* Champaign, IL: Stipes Publishing.

Author's Description. This book presents a series of articles on an approach to change known as Appreciative Inquiry, or AI for short. AI is an approach, which in its brief lifetime has made considerable impact on the field of Organizational Development. It provides a critical new way of thinking about organizational change and improvement, yet at the same time is deeply rooted in the historical values of OD. Appreciative Inquiry draws on the best of "what is" and envisioning, and consequently creates what is at the heart of OD, which is perhaps best expressed by Marvin Weisbord as *the creation of productive workplaces with dignity, meaning, and community....* AI has been recognized by many OD professional associations, including as Award for Best Organizations Change Program from the American Society for Training and Development. It was part of the change effort that won the Outstanding OD Project of the Year Worldwide from the OD Institute, and was the topic of one of the articles selected and published as "The Best of the OD Journal in the 20th Century," and a special issue of the *OD Practitioner* published by OD Network.

Setting, Purpose, and Benefit. AI has been used within organizations to unleash enthusiasm, creativity, and grassroots initiative. The foundation of AI is to ask individuals to identify examples in their organization of when things have worked well, when their organization has been most alive and effective, and then to inquire about what allowed this to happen. AI is led by a trained facilitator who prepares individual and group inquiries based on a vision of the desired future. This desired future expands forward the organization at its best. AI requires participation from the organization leadership and a willingness to unleash the individual energies of all the employees without trying to overly control or squash the outcomes.

Problem-solving methods of change often devolve into defensiveness, erosion of energy, hopelessness, and loss of personal power. A deficit model asks, "What is wrong, what is the problem, or what is not working?" The question asked at the start determines what is found and either inspires or deflates life energy. Contrary to some approaches, AI does not start off by identifying problems. Instead, AI starts by asking "What do you want more of?" and builds a vision of the future based on that. AI works within the organization in "constructive, positive, life-affirming, even spiritual ways."

AI theory says that organizations are networks of human relationships. These relationships thrive when people see the best in each other and share a positive dream, and when they are empowered to create this dream together. Therefore, an AI intervention creates a visionary change initiative from the organization-wide, grassroots, positive experiences of the employees and management that takes on a power, energy, and life of its own. "As people throughout a system connect in serious study into qualities, examples, and analysis of the positive core – each appreciating and everyone being appreciated – hope grows and community expands." Examples of AI interventions indicate the enormous capacity they have to release human energy and creativity beyond what is typically seen in conventional problem-solving or bureaucratic change initiatives.

Basic Procedure. AI interventions follow four steps: discovery, dream, design, and destiny.

1. *Discovery*. Employees are trained to interview other employees to gather examples of the organization at its best and most alive. The interviewees are then asked to interview more employees until a critical mass of employees have been interviewed and their stories have been compiled. Facilitators use these stories to develop a set of envisioning questions about what the future of the organization would look like in five years. These questions are specific to the qualities that characterize the organization at its best.

2. *Dream*. The questions generated from the data collected in Discovery are used in Step Two in a large group workshop. Everyone in the organization is invited to attend the workshop and participate in small group discussions and whole group sharing about their dreams for the organization. These dreams usually coalesce around a few key areas.

3. *Design*. The participants of the workshop begin to design the systems and structures needed in order to fulfill the shared vision for the organization identified in Step Two. The nature of the design is based on networks of communication, partnership, and cooperation rather than bureaucratic or hierarchical structures. The Dream and Design steps are grounded in the stories of examples where the organization has already demonstrated capacity for positive outcomes and expands on what already exists.

4. *Destiny*. This step involves planning for "continuous learning, adjustment, and improvisation in the service of shared ideals." The Destiny step addresses issues of implementation and sustainability. In this step, the momentum and power for change is given away to everyone. It is not packaged and put on the shelf but instead people are empowered to become a movement. Participants develop an action plan that is designed to have a momentum of its own through 1) network-like struc-

tures that connect and empower people and 2) "convergence zones" where employees share breakthroughs and have opportunities to cooperate, co-create, and celebrate each other.

Dynamic Facilitation

Worldcat Reference. Zubizarreta, R. (2014). *From conflict to creative collaboration: A user's guide to Dynamic Facilitation.* Minneapolis, MN: Two Harbors.

Author's Description. A detailed user's guide for organizational consultants, facilitators, and mediators. As group facilitators, we can use methods like Open Space Technology, Future Search, and World Café to reliably evoke "group magic" when working with larger groups. Yet how can we tap into the generative power of self-organization when working with smaller groups -- especially ones facing complex and conflict-laden issues?

In *From Conflict to Creative Collaboration: A User's Guide to Dynamic Facilitation,* collaboration consultant Rosa Zubizarreta introduces a highly effective and agile way to welcome task groups into a co-creative "flow zone" -- where participants create practical and innovative solutions while building trust, empathy, and authentic community. Zubizarreta describes a ground-breaking facilitation approach for transforming unproductive group friction into world-class teamwork and innovation, which will allow them to be more effective at drawing out group creativity.

Setting, Purpose, and Benefit. Dynamic Facilitation is intended for small group dialogue, between 5-20 people ideally. Its primary purpose is "choice-creating" leading to a practical way of responding to a particular problem that works for everyone in an expansive way rather than through compromise. Dynamic Facilitation does not require any skills on the part of the partici-pants in order to engage in this protocol. The trained facilitator is active in terms of facilitating the conversation, and non-directive, in terms of content. The facilitator welcomes participant advocacy on whatever issue is of most concern to them at the moment, actively draws out each contribution, and provides a safe space for group process and transformation.

All ideas are recorded on chart paper in numbered lists. As each participant is fully heard, they are free to expand their thinking and to launch off of other's ideas. New possibilities begin to emerge from the collective contributions of the group as the map of ideas expands. The facilitator welcomes divergent ideas for their value in stimulating creativity. However, the facilitator does not encourage interpersonal confrontation. The facilitator, as the designated listener, is the recipient of all contributions which are recorded immediately for all to see.

Dynamic Facilitation differs from some other protocols by welcoming initial solutions, concerns about those solutions, and even alternative definitions of the initial problem. The purpose of Dynamic Facilitation is to help participants develop a common understanding of the larger system in which the problem is embedded as well as to consider multiple perspectives and concerns that are relevant for the ultimate solutions. Plans for action generally emerge naturally from the process and are readily embraced by all who are present because they have already been thoroughly vetted by the process.

Basic Procedure.

1. The facilitator actively manages the interactions but not the content. Through modeling, (rather than by articulating fixed ground rules) the facilitator listens intently to one person at a time and reflects fully. If people begin to speak to each other, the facilitator will gently direct all communication to her/himself. This process creates safety for the group, slows down the conversation so that people can listen more deeply, and fully allows each individual to contribute their perspective.

2. The facilitator works with that one person until the participant is satisfied that their idea has been fully heard and correctly recorded on one of the flip charts. The facilitator then asks this same person for a possible solution and records this on the appropriate flip chart.

3. Flip Charts are labeled with one of four categories per chart: Problem Statements, Solutions, Concerns, or Data/Perspectives and the facilitator works with the individual speaker to determine where to place their input.

4. The facilitator then engages with the next person who wants to share their perspective about the issue.

5. Facilitators follow the group in terms of content and do not try to lead the group to agreement or action planning. The facilitator listens to and records whatever emerges in the moment. If the facilitator leads at all, it is to encourage people to express divergent perspectives to make sure that every perspective is heard and that no one is holding back.

6. While facilitators do not lead a group through stages, the group process tends to follow a consistent pattern: Purge stage, Yuck stage, Flow stage, and Commitment stage.

7. *Purge Stage* is the starting place where people share what they already know about the issue and potential solutions they have already thought about. Facilitators begin by inviting the recognized leader to start by sharing her/his perspective and any favored solutions, decisions, or constraints from the leader's perspective. This is followed by the facilitator inviting, listening to, and recording all the other perspectives, concerns, and possible solutions among the participants.

8. *Yuck Stage* is a very short transition from the Purge Stage to the Flow Stage where participants are faced with the enormity

of the problem, may feel stuck or overwhelmed with the apparent impossibility of a solution, and are faced with the seeming conflict among the various perspectives. The task of the facilitator at this stage is to resist rescuing the group. This discomfort is the motivation for the emergence of creativity which quickly follows.

9. *Flow Stage* begins when the first person tentatively proposes something new and possibilities begin to emerge from the group taking on a flow of excitement and creative energy. The Flow Stage is characterized by an on-going cycle of divergence, to convergence, to divergence as each new possibility throws light on a new problem.

10. *Commitment Stage.* At some point, and without any push from the facilitator, the group begins to sense a meeting of the minds and readiness to recognize clear action steps that have emerged from the process. Someone may call for a commitment to action, signaling they have reached the Commitment Stage. Contrary to the more familiar decision making process, Dynamic Facilitation creates convergence without it ever being discussed in the recognized pattern of formal decision making. And yet, everyone is in agreement because the facilitator has made sure that any divergence has been brought to the surface in the Purge and Flow stages. This meeting of the minds or breakthrough is what Dynamic Facilitation is designed to elicit by bringing forward the diversity of perspectives, listening fully to each perspective, reflecting back what is heard, and trusting that the group will self-organize to find its own path forward as a result of the process.

Wisdom Council

Worldcat Reference. Zubizarreta, R. (2014). *From conflict to creative collaboration: A user's guide to Dynamic Facilitation.* Minneapolis, MN: Two Harbors.

Author's Description. A detailed user's guide for organizational consultants, facilitators, and mediators. As group facilitators, we can use methods like Open Space Technology, Future Search, and World Café to reliably evoke "group magic" when working with larger groups. Yet how can we tap into the generative power of self-organization when working with smaller groups -- especially ones facing complex and conflict-laden issues?

In *From Conflict to Creative Collaboration: A User's Guide to Dynamic Facilitation,* collaboration consultant Rosa Zubizarreta introduces a highly effective and agile way to welcome task groups into a co-creative "flow zone"—where participants create practical and innovative solutions while building trust, empathy, and authentic community. Zubizarreta describes a ground-breaking facilitation approach for transforming unproductive group friction into world-class teamwork and innovation, which will allow them to be more effective at drawing out group creativity.

Setting, Purpose, and Benefit. Wisdom Council is a particular application of Dynamic Facilitation that is worthy of individual attention, particularly for use within a larger system. The Wisdom Council protocol solves a specific problem of transferring the experience and creative breakthroughs of a small group back into the larger organization. This protocol can help to overcome the "not created here" barrier of wisdom-transference. If you have ever suffered the frustration of working diligently with a representative group on solving a problem, only to have it rejected when presented to the organization as a whole, then the Wisdom Council protocol may provide an alternative process.

The intention of the Wisdom Council protocol is to build a conscious awareness of deeper issues within the organization, to engage people in constructive "choice-creating" conversations, and to build a sense of inclusion, participation, and agency within the larger system. The stories from participants of this transformative experience begin to plant seeds within the organization as a whole. Rather than arriving from a small group experience with a finished end-product and an expectation that the rest of the organization will receive it with open arms, this protocol presents seeds of thoughtful process that spread throughout the organization on a repeated basis. As a regular practice, this protocol serves to deepen the level of conversation and creative problem solving within the entire organization.

Basic Procedure.

1. Periodically bring together a small, representative group of the whole organization. Each time, the group should include a wide diversity of perspectives within the different individuals invited to participate. Each gathering should be with a completely new set of individuals.

2. The small group participates in a two-day intensive Dynamic Facilitation process where the only agenda is to discuss what each individual sees as the significant issues currently facing the larger organization. The process is facilitated using the same protocol discussed above under Dynamic Facilitation.

3. The last step of this "Intensive" is to identify areas of convergence that have emerged during the process and to summarize the final outcome of the group.

4. The group then presents their outcomes to a general assembly of the whole organization by sharing their stories about their experience in the Intensive.

5. The entire organization is invited to consider the outcomes and continue the conversation within the broader community.

6. This process is repeated at regular intervals with a new group.

World Café

Worldcat Reference. Brown, J., & Isaacs, D. (2005). *The World Café: Shaping our futures through conversations that matter.* San Francisco, CA: Berrett-Koehler Publishers.

Author's Description. The World Café process has been used by tens of thousands of people around the world to tackle real-life issues. Based on seven key principles, it begins with small, intimate conversations at café-style tables; these gatherings then link and build on each other as people move between groups and cross-pollinate ideas. In this way, Café learning enables even very large groups to think together creatively in a single, connected conversation. This complete resource explains the Café concept and provides readers with the tools they need to get started. Each chapter opens with stories from business, education, government, and community organizations, each a dramatic example of how leaders are using this process in the real world. Such stories underline the Café's immediate, practical implications for meeting and conference design, strategy formation, knowledge creation, and large-scale systems change. The book includes a foreword by best-selling author Margaret J. Wheatley, an afterword by author Peter Senge, and real-world stories of the Café process in action at Hewlett-Packard, the nation of Singapore, and the University of Texas.

Setting, Purpose, and Benefit. World Café has been held for groups ranging in size from 12 to 1,200 and may be held for half a day or even one week. World Café dialogues have been held around the world with businesses, government entities, communities, special gatherings, board retreats, strategic planning sessions, faculty groups from multiple countries and universities to discuss issues such as sustainable development, distance education, creating innovative technologies, and community collaboration. The goal of a World Café dialogue is to support "productive relationships, collaborative learning, and collective insight around real-life challenges and key strategic questions." World Café is particularly useful for creating an environment which supports cross-pollination of ideas.

World Café has many similarities to the other emergent protocols already discussed. However, World Café has a special flare that definitely signals that a new protocol is operating. World Café protocol can have many variations on the process outlined below to fit different groups and topics. However, cross-pollination of ideas across small groups is a common element. World Café is based on the idea that conversation is a generative force as we "speak our world into existence through conversations that matter." The World Café protocol can generate shared ideas and perspectives that can be put into action.

Similar to the other emergent protocols, there must be a receptive rather than authoritarian context for the conversation. The World Café protocol is not advised for topics that are potentially conflictual or highly emotional where a skilled facilitator would be required. Facilitating a World Café protocol is more like hosting than facilitation. Special facilitation training is not necessary; however, strong hosting and connecting skills would be very helpful in creating a welcoming and relaxed environment. Some advanced planning is required in terms of 1) identifying questions that matter and are interesting and engaging for the attendees, 2) identifying and inviting participants, and 3) logistics for setting up the room and gathering supplies.

The World Café protocol has been used in formal and informal settings. It can be used as a follow-on activity to an invited speaker. It can be used as regular part of a system-wide leadership meeting to provide focused time to talk together about things that matter instead of just the usual business agenda. It can also be used in a planning meeting to identify the key questions to ask in a larger Café dialogue. The questions posed in a World Café protocol are important for the success of the dialogue. Here are just a few examples of possible questions to give you an idea of the flavor of the conversation.

- What could make the greatest difference to the situation we are exploring?
- What dilemmas/opportunities can we see in this situation?
- What assumptions do we need to test about this situation?
- What do we already know about this situation and what additional information do we need?
- Who might have a very different perspective about this situation and what might they say?

Basic Procedure.

Seven Design Principles

1. Set the context by clarifying the purpose and parameters of the dialogue.
2. Create hospitable space to ensure a welcoming and safe environment. This protocol gets its name from the typical café-like set-up of small tables with 4-5 chairs, paper table-cloths, sprigs of fresh flowers on each table, and attractive decorations like plants and posters. Food and drinks are freely available throughout the event to sustain a café-like atmosphere.
3. Explore questions that matter.
4. Encourage everyone's participation regardless of status or position in the system.

5. Cross-pollinate and connect diverse perspectives.

6. Invite participants to listen for patterns, insights, and deeper questions.

7. Share collective discoveries and insights with the whole group.

Assumptions

1. The knowledge and wisdom we need are already present and accessible.

2. Intelligence emerges as the system connects to itself in creative ways.

3. Collective insight evolves from a) honoring unique contributions, b) connecting ideas, c) listening into the middle, and d) noticing deeper patterns and questions.

Etiquette

1. Contribute your thinking and experience
2. Listen to understand

3. Connect ideas

4. Listen together for patterns, insights, and deeper questions

5. Play, doodle, draw!

Process Steps

1. The Café Host introduces the event including the principles, assumptions, etiquette, and the process. The Host presents the purpose and the question topic for the Café.

2. Each table of four or five people has a table host who volunteers to remain at that table. The table host engages in the conversation as a participant rather than as a facilitator. In addition, the table host shares the essence of the ongoing

conversation that has occurred at this table with each new set of "guests."

3. The dialogue is organized in a series of "rounds" of progressive conversation, with each round lasting about 30 minutes. When a round ends, the guests of each table move to a new table to sit with a completely different set of people.

4. Everyone at the table supports the table host by taking notes, summarizing, and making drawings/charts on the sheet of newsprint paper covering the table. These notes support the host in sharing the key ideas that have emerged with the next set of guests.

5. Guests traveling to new tables in the next round carry the themes, key ideas, patterns, questions, and insights to the next table conversation, thus "cross-pollinating" the conversations in each round. When it is not physically possible for people to move to a new table, the main ideas, patterns, and questions from the table can be written on index cards which are passed to a new table.

6. As a new round begins with a new set of people at each table, the table host begins by summarizing the conversation that has occurred at this table. Guests then add relevant connections and ideas from the different conversations at their previous tables. The members then build on the conversation from there. The Café Host may periodically remind each table to ask, "What is at the center of our conversation?"

7. The Café Host may introduce a new question at the start of a round to stimulate the conversation in a specific direction. The progression of questions is planned prior to the start of the Café to meet the specific purpose of the dialogue.

8. After the planned number of Café rounds have occurred, the whole group engages in one conversation to reflect on what has emerged as a result of the progressive rounds. The Café Host may begin the whole-group conversation by asking one person to share a key idea, theme, or question that has real meaning to them. The Café Host then encourages other participants to share how their conversation links to this initial sharing. This process is repeated so that each newly presented idea is connected to ideas that have emerged in other groups. This process of linking ideas is therefore different from the common process of reporting by groups. Key insights from this whole-group conversation are recorded visually and posted for everyone to see.

Last Words

I believe that having knowledge about different forms of conversations and creating the conditions necessary to implement them are among the most needed skills in our world today. By cultivating this skill we can increase the possibility of creating environments where it is safe to speak authentically and to collaborate in finding solutions to our biggest challenges. Any of the protocols discussed in this book, as well as others that have not been specifically mentioned, can be the start of changing both small and big systems from families to communities, schools, and government; changing dialogues about religion, race, environment, and politics; and changing national and global relationships.

When I read stories about the kinds of conversations that these protocols have generated, I feel energized and hopeful about what we can accomplish when we communicate and collaborate together. A key element that is often missing in our communication in groups is a positive protocol that sets the purpose and tone for the conversation and establishes the rules to the game that promote deep listening, acceptance of diverse perspectives, creativity, collaboration, and shared insight. The authors of these protocols have already successfully demonstrated that we can accomplish a shift in the nature of our group dialogues, even in difficult, challenging or seemingly impossible circumstances. We *can* do it. My hope is that you feel empowered and inspired by the examples in this book and that you will find opportunities to implement a new protocol somewhere in your life, thereby changing the world one conversation at a time.

Harmony World Publishing

Harmony World Publishing is dedicated to facilitating the development of world peace and the advancement of human communication and relationships through publishing books, articles, blogs, and other written materials. The Japanese word for harmony, Aiki, is the ability to harmonize with an opponent's energy and is one of the essential qualities for a traditional Japanese warrior. This principle of Aiki is essential in political, business, and social leaders as well as in families, schools, and social activism. The promotion of world harmony requires strength, commitment, inner discipline, and courage. Harmony is the opposite of domination of one person, group, or idea over another. The ability to relate effectively with people of diverse cultures and perspectives is a hallmark of harmony as is the ability to find solutions through collaboration and dialogue that meet everyone's needs. There is a need in our world for increasing the skills of people at all levels to facilitate peace building activities and communication. To this end, Harmony World Publishing promotes materials that support the development of understanding and skillfulness in facilitating peace.

website: www.harmonyworld.net

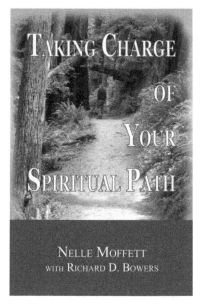

Taking Charge of Your Spiritual Path. For both those who have found a spiritual home and for those who are still looking, there is a need for spiritual seekers to have a better understanding of the process and principles of spiritual development. If you want to do practices that have meaning for you and to be able to change your practice when something more or different is needed, this book will provide you with some basic principles to help you take charge of your own spiritual path. People are taking more responsibility for managing their own finances, their own psychological well-being, and their own education. Likewise, it is possible now to take charge of one's own spiritual path. In most spiritual paths, the outcomes are often not made clear and the focus is placed on the practice itself without making the objective of the practice clear. This is disempowering for you, the practitioner. But now, we no longer have to stay stuck in this model. The purpose of this book is to identify some common underlying objectives of true spiritual practices outside of the doctrine that surrounds them. This book discusses the specific outcomes that different practices are designed to accomplish. ISBN 978-0-9911-1171-8

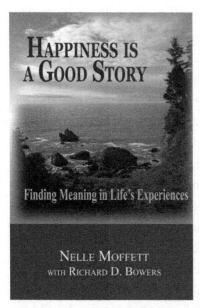

Happiness is a Good Story: Finding Meaning in Life's Experiences. This book uses many personal stories and examples to describe how you can create more happiness in your life through becoming aware of your meaning-making process. Our personal stories shape our lives. Human beings were designed to create stories, make meaning, and interpret the world we perceive. This ability to make meaning defines our humanity as opposed to animals or plants. Our stories about ourselves and others are the meaning that we have made up to make sense of something that happened. However, our suffering also lies primarily in the meaning that we give to what happened. If we assign the meaning to what happened, then we also are empowered to change the meaning that we create. To regain our empowerment, we have an opportunity to create stories that open up new possibilities, "reframe" a situation, or re-tell our story to our self from a different framework. This book provides specific examples for how to transform your meaning-making process from one that is disempowering to one that empowers you as the hero of your own story. ISBN 978-0-9911-1170-1

...the Professional Series

EMPATHY IN
CONFLICT
INTERVENTION

THE KEY TO SUCCESSFUL NVC MEDIATION

RICHARD D. BOWERS
NELLE MOFFETT

Empathy in Conflict Intervention: The Key to Successful NVC Mediation. The focus of this book is on mediation, a third party intervention role that can be undertaken by supervisors, managers, human resource professionals, marriage and family therapists, teachers, mediators, peace keepers, and parents. The authors make a strong case for the central role of empathy in promoting a successful mediation, especially when ongoing relationships between the parties are at stake. This book provides a thoughtful study of the important role of empathy in mediation through the development of a theoretical model to explain the effectiveness of Nonviolent Communication™ (NVC) mediation. The theory building process used in this book, as well as the list of conditions for a successful mediation, can be broadly applied to other third party intervention methods. ISBN 978-1-4776-1460-0

About the Authors

 Nelle Moffett and Rick Bowers are married to each other and have a consulting company, Speak Peace, through which they lead workshops, facilitate practice groups and coach individuals, parents, couples, and businesses in communication and conflict resolution using Marshall Rosenberg's Nonviolent Communication™.

Nelle Moffett, Ph.D., spent 25 years in higher education as a strategic planner, researcher, change agent, coach, and internal consultant. She received her doctoral degree in Educational Leadership and Policy Studies from Arizona State University. She has taught Psychology courses at California State University Channel Islands. Nelle is a certified Life Coach and certified teacher of Inner Relationship Focusing. Nelle received training in communication skills from Landmark Education and the Center for Nonviolent Communication. Nelle is a long-time student of life, spirituality, philosophy and psychology.

Email: moffett@speak-peace.com.

Rick Bowers, M.A., Rick spent twenty-six years with Hewlett-Packard Company, primarily in Research and Development. In 2007 he left Hewlett-Packard to obtain a Master's Degree in Conflict Analysis and Engagement at Antioch University Midwest. He has mediated in the courts in Ventura and LA counties in California. Rick received training in communication skills from Landmark Education and the Center for Nonviolent Communication.

Email: bowers@speak-peace.com

Made in the USA
Las Vegas, NV
19 November 2021